Social media Techniques for Small business

Ishaku Mafeng

Table of contents

Presentation

Small business techniques

1. Pick the Right Organizations

2. Put forth an Objective

3. Think of a Strategy

4. Make a Substance Creation or Curation

5. Select Apparatuses to Timetable and Computerize Posts

6. Effectively Connect with Your Crowd in Applicable Ways

7. Limit the Time You Spend Advancing

8. Keep a Steady Presence and Brand Voice

9. Watch the Right Measurements to Screen Your Advancement

10. Continue advancing by signing up for social media and showcasing the course

11. Evaluate your opposition

copyright © by Ishaku Mafeng 2023. All rights reserved.

Before this document is duplicated or reproduced in any manner, the publisher's consent must be gained. Therefore, the contents within can neither be stored electronically, transferred, nor kept in a database. Neither in Part nor full can the document be copied, scanned, faxed, or retained without approval from the publisher or creator.

Presentation

Concerning social media achievement, a tiny amount of arranging makes a huge difference. Fostering major areas of strength for a media technique for small businesses will take out a ton of the mystery from your promoting endeavors and guarantee that the time and assets you contribute convey the best return.

The viability of social media advertising is irrefutable; the issue is deciding how to zero in on it when financial plans and individuals are restricted. The critical switches for laying out areas of strength for a media presence for your small business are to realize who you're conversing with, layout objectives, center around the right stages, investigate your opposition, and cautiously send your assets by figuring out where they will have the best effect.

Small business techniques

Small businesses all over the planet realize that social media is staying put. You just have to take a gander at the social media socioeconomics across stages to know that! However, that doesn't mean you have gotten the opportunity to invest the energy or exertion important to develop a legitimate presence in the right organizations.

Regardless of whether you haven't improved your social media presence, there's time, and the advantages will merit the work. There are many benefits to developing your image on social media. It can assist with further developing your image's social client care, permit you to speak with clients and possibilities on another level, help draw in and contact new crowds, fabricate authority, and direct people to your site.

To put it plainly, making a viable social media procedure can drive development for your small business by cultivating enduring and faithful associations with possibilities and clients. To guarantee your image's presence on social media is made with quality and consistency, utilize a social media style manual to monitor a wide range of components.

1. Pick the Right Organizations

Social media has exploded since Facebook opened up to the world back in 2012, and there is a large number of organizations devoted to anything from associating old schoolmates to social activism.

So with this multitude of choices, how does a business pick the right ones? The guidance from most specialists is to join the most famous, and picking the right ones descends to your crowd and your objectives. Here is data to assist with kicking you off:

Facebook: the biggest stage, has 2.89 billion dynamic month-to-month clients, and the site is great for businesses that need to produce leads and fabricate connections.

LinkedIn: the stage for business systems administration can be utilized by both B2B and B2C businesses to make trust, construct authority, and draw in crowds.

Twitter: whose stage is immediacy, is ideally suited for businesses whose significant crowd is under 50 and who need to keep steady over time-delicate data like making it known, declarations, and moving themes.

Pinterest: the photo-sharing site, is an incredible stage for businesses with visual allure (think cafés, style, craftsmanship, travel, and weddings). It's more for social disclosure than social systems administration and is perfect for driving deals because countless clients shift focus over to the site to design buys.

Snapchat: the terminating content stage, is one of the quickest developing social systems administration locales despite bits of gossip about the parent organization Snap being in a difficult situation a couple of years prior. Businesses can use Snapchat by offering advancements, giving customized content, giving select access, and building associations with powerhouses to drive memorability and dependability.

Instagram: Instagram was effective to the point that only 2 years after sending off it was purchased by Facebook, in 2012. Its prosperity is attached to remaining consistent with its unique objective - permitting clients to post photographs and recordings from their versatile. The formation of Instagram Stories (a thought taken from Snapchat!) highlighting content that terminates in 24 hours has empowered it to hoard almost 1 billion worldwide clients.

TikTok: A peculiarity in the social media world, TikTok is an amazing powerhouse, seeing fast development during the Coronavirus pandemic. It is the first application not possessed by Facebook to have arrived at 3 billion installs because of its ubiquity among powerhouses and big names. The convenience of the stage, tremendous music index and remarkable channels draw in a connection with the more youthful segment.

2. Put forth an Objective

Being dynamic on social media has various advantages for your business, and there are numerous things you can achieve with a social presence. This incorporates performing client support, connecting with clients, producing leads, growing your crowd, driving deals, expanding web traffic, acquiring significant experiences and input, and considerably more.

Yet, to accomplish these with any proportion of progress, you should have an objective to pursue since you'll have to do whatever it may take to think up a social media strategy and arrive. Your procedures for driving deals, for example, will be unique in your way to deal with further developing your client support offering. So it's essential to understand what you need to achieve.

3. Think of a Strategy

Having an objective for further developing your social media presence is perfect, yet at the same, it's just the start. When you understand what you need to accomplish, you need to concoct an arrangement to arrive.

Begin by assigning the individual or individuals who will be important for the social media group, and separate their jobs and obligations so everyone realizes what's generally anticipated and when.
You must likewise settle on your posting always, make a posting schedule that will help you with organizing posts and don't miss days. This way to deal with a booking is a major piece of your strategy and there are extraordinary social media schedule formats you can utilize that spread out:

1. who is your crowd is

2. What points and subjects your crowd is keen on

3. The usable substance you as of now have

4. What sort of satisfied you need to make or arrange

5. When and at what stages content will be distributed

6. The best method for fostering a strategy for your business is to gain from the best. Consider a social media and showcasing course that spotlights social examination and social strategy so you track down your crowd and skill to connect with them.

4. Make a Substance Creation or Curation

Understanding what your listeners might be thinking is basic concerning making progress with social media commitment. This is because the interests and needs of your crowd will decide the sort of happiness you ought to share and how you draw in your adherents.

For example, if you're an espresso roastery, your interest group may be keen on recipes for extravagant natural product drinks, blending tips and methods, and other natural product-related articles. A portion of the significant things you ought to understand where your listeners might be coming from incorporate age, area, orientation, objectives, likes, needs, ways of behaving, difficulties, and trouble spots.

Regardless of who your crowd is, the substance you offer ought to continuously be excellent and applicable. You ought to examine the famous substance types and focus on the record, pictures, and different kinds of visual substance as frequently as conceivable because these are inclined toward all socioeconomics and crowds.

5. Select Apparatuses to Timetable and Computerize Posts

Remaining dynamic and present on social media takes time and commitment. In any case, there are a lot of computerization devices accessible to content makers to distribute and plan presents a month ahead of time naturally.

These apparatuses, which incorporate Hootsuite, Fledgling Social, Cushion, MeetEdgar, and BuzzSumo, can save you time by permitting you to plan and timetable bunches of posts without a moment's delay. They additionally make it more straightforward to screen your organizations and answer messages rapidly.

6. Effectively Connect with Your Crowd in Applicable Ways

Albeit content is especially significant on social media, it's sufficient not to simply post your substance and leave. You need to make content that invigorates and engages to interface and drive commitment. That way you can encourage the connections you need to fabricate and acquire the trust of your crowd.

There are numerous ways you can draw in your crowds:

1. Remark on posts

2. Begin and partake in discussions

3. Share significant data

4. Share client-produced content (UGC)

5. Ask and address inquiries

6. Post questions circle back to the results

7. Address protests and reactions

8. Show appreciation for clients

7. Limit the Time You Spend Advancing

Albeit the act of social offering to expand deals is turning out to be progressively well known among sales reps and advertisers, the method involved with utilizing social organizations to drive development is not quite the same as what a great many people are utilized to. Instead of involving social as a functioning limited-time stage, involving it as an instrument for commitment and communication is ideal.

It's suggested that businesses follow the 80/20 rule and keep their limited-time content to 20%. The vast majority of content ought to be committed to addressing the necessities of your crowd.

8. Keep a Steady Presence and Brand Voice

Social media is certainly not a limited-time offer arrangement. It requires investment and persistence to develop a dependable presence.

In an ideal stage for brand building and acknowledgment, each post must be following your image and picture. This can become troublesome assuming you have different individuals appointed to social media since everyone will carry their character to their posts. For this explanation, it's ideal to restrict the number of individuals liable for posting and ensure everybody knows the voice and picture you need to introduce.

With regards to posting, robotization devices utilized successfully can save you a ton of time and guarantee your presence in your organizations in any event, when you're not! With the right devices, you can limit the time you need to devote to social media, yet will in any case expect no less than 15 minutes per day to screen your channels and answer questions.

As far as posting is regular, the right number truly relies upon the stage you're using. For LinkedIn and Facebook, don't post at least a few times per day, and limit your presence to five times each week. Twitter, then again, changes so rapidly that the more you post, the better.

9. Watch the Right Measurements to Screen Your Advancement

Social media use is developing constantly, and each month there are more dynamic clients than the one preceding, particularly on well-known networks. Having a presence on each social stage out there is excessive. It's a vastly improved strategy to characterize your objectives, find your crowd, and pick the organizations that are ideal for you in light of those variables.

Your image abilities and social media objectives will decide the measurements that matter and it's essential to gauge these to guarantee you're doing great. For example, to increment site traffic, then, at that point, focus on how much reference traffic comes from social.

There are numerous assets you can depend on for measurements, including Google Investigation, Facebook Examination and page bits of knowledge, Fledgling Social, LinkedIn organization pages report, Keyhole, Twitter examination and catchphrase reports, Cradle, and BuzzSumo.

10. Continue advancing by signing up for social media and showcasing the course

The way to dominate social media is to comprehend how to find and connect with your crowd and how every stage functions. An extraordinary method for doing this is to require some investment to sign up for a social media and showcasing course that will show you all that you want to be aware of to drive business achievement.

11. Evaluate your opposition

A fundamental piece of a social media strategy for small businesses is looking at your opposition's social presence. There are two justifications for why contender surveys are significant:

The exhibition of your rivals on stage explicit channels can be a marker concerning whether it's a stage worth utilizing for your own small business.

Investigating their substance (great and terrible) can likewise assist with impacting your ideas. The thought here isn't to simply recreate a contender's substance strategy. All things being equal, you ought to do a contender survey. The objective is to figure out what types of content work and which ones don't. This can assist you with grasping a contender's assets and restrictions, as well as what individuals expect from a brand in your equivalent region.

www.ingramcontent.com/pod-product-compliance
Lightning Source LLC
Chambersburg PA
CBHW070322220526
45465CB00013B/2184